The Hole Truth!
Underground Animal Life

Badger's Burrow

by Dee Phillips

Consultants:

Josh Sayers
Ontario Badger Project

Kimberly Brenneman, PhD
National Institute for Early Education Research, Rutgers University, New Brunswick, New Jersey

BEARPORT
PUBLISHING

New York, New York

Credits

Cover ©Donald M. Jones/Minden Pictures/FLPA, ©Minden Pictures/Superstock, ©Subbotina Anna/Shutterstock, ©Menna/ Shutterstock and ©Potapov Alexander/Shutterstock; 4T, ©Josh Sayers; 4B, ©Tom Vezo/Minden Pictures/FLPA; 5, ©Minden Pictures/ Superstock; 6T, ©visceralimage/Shutterstock; 6B, ©Cosmographics; 7, ©Donald M. Jones/Minden Pictures/FLPA; 8, ©Sylvain Cordier/ Biosphoto/FLPA; 9, ©Zeljko Radojko/Shutterstock and ©Minden Pictures/Superstock; 10, ©Jonathunder/Wikipedia Creative Commons; 11, ©age fotostock/Superstock; 12, ©Michael Quinton/Minden Pictures/FLPA; 13, ©Gerald A. DeBoer/Shutterstock, ©Gerald Marella/ Shutterstock, ©Sergey Goruppa/Shutterstock, ©fivespots/Shutterstock, ©Allocricetulus/Shutterstock, ©Dimj/Shutterstock and Terry Reimink/Shutterstock; 14–15, ©Donald M. Jones/Minden Pictures/FLPA; 16, ©Ernest Wilkinson/Animals Animals; 18, ©H. Reinhard/ Arco Images/Alamy; 19, ©franzfoto.com/Alamy; 20, ©Donald M. Jones/Minden Pictures/FLPA; 21, ©Paul Sawer/FLPA; 22, ©Morales/ age fotostock/Superstock, ©Xavier Marchant/Shutterstock, ©imagebroker.net/Superstock, ©artcphotos/Shutterstock, ©igorsky/ Shutterstock, ©Cynthia Kidwell/Shutterstock and ©Konrad Wothe/Minden Pictures/FLPA; 23TL, ©Josh Sayers; 23TC, ©outdoorsman/ Shutterstock and ©Minden Pictures/Superstock; 23TR, ©Jupiter Images/Thinkstock; 23BL, ©Artens/Shutterstock; 23BC, ©worldswildlifewonders/Shutterstock; 23BR, ©visceralimage/Shutterstock.

Publisher: Kenn Goin
Editorial Director: Adam Siegel
Editor: Joy Bean
Creative Director: Spencer Brinker
Design: Alix Wood
Editor: Mark J. Sachner
Photo Researcher: Ruby Tuesday Books Ltd

Library of Congress Cataloging-in-Publication Data in process at time of publication (2013)
Library of Congress Control Number: 2012040429
ISBN-13: 978-1-61772-745-0 (library binding)

For more information, write to Bearport Publishing Company, Inc., 45 West 21st Street, Suite 3B, New York, New York 10010. Printed in the United States of America.

10 9 8 7 6 5 4 3 2 1

Contents

A Badger's Hiding Place

It is early evening, and the sun will go down soon.

Suddenly, a striped face peeks out of a hole at the edge of a meadow.

It's an American badger, and the hole is the entrance to its **burrow**.

burrow

All day, the badger has been asleep in its underground hiding place.

Now, it is wide-awake and ready to spend the night searching for food.

4

burrow
entrance

Badgers sleep, hide from enemies, and raise their babies in their burrows.

American badger

What do you think the inside of a badger's burrow looks like?

Check Out a Badger

Badgers belong to the same animal family as otters and weasels.

They are chunky animals with wide, flat bodies and short legs.

They have thick, gray hair on their bodies and grayish-brown and white striped faces.

Badgers dig burrows in open, grassy places such as **prairies** and meadows.

striped face

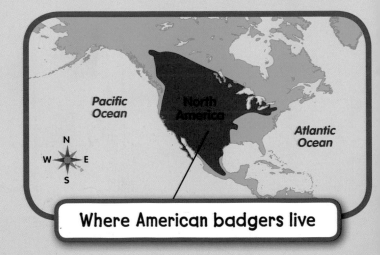

Pacific Ocean

North America

Atlantic Ocean

N
W — E
S

Where American badgers live

An adult badger is about 25 inches (64 cm) long from its nose to the tip of its tail.

Look at this picture of a badger. How do you think the animal makes its burrow?

Welcome to a Badger's Burrow

Badgers dig their burrows using the long claws on their front feet.

A badger begins work by making an entrance hole.

The hardworking animal digs and loosens the soil with its front claws.

Then it kicks the loose soil out of the hole with its back feet.

The badger digs a long tunnel.

Then, at the end of the tunnel, it makes a cozy bedroom.

a badger digging with its claws

Try to guess how many burrows a badger has in the area where it lives.

cornfield

entrance hole

A badger's bedroom may be up to 10 feet (3 m) underground.

tunnel

bedroom

Sleepy Days, Busy Nights

Badgers are **nocturnal** animals, which means they are mostly awake at night.

During the day, a badger sleeps in its burrow.

At night, it leaves its burrow and may walk many miles looking for food.

In the morning, when it is ready to sleep, it finds one of its burrows.

A badger may have hundreds of burrows in the area where it lives!

a badger inside its burrow

a badger trying to scare an enemy

If an enemy, such as a bear or wolf, comes close, a badger hides in a burrow. Sometimes a badger cannot get to a hiding place. Then the badger shows its teeth and tries to scare the bigger animal.

Badger Food

Badgers are meat eaters that feed on small animals.

They spend the night hunting for **prey** such as groundhogs, chipmunks, and ground squirrels.

All these small creatures live in burrows that are too small for badgers to fit into.

That's not a problem, however, because badgers have a special way to catch their prey.

duck eggs

Badgers sometimes eat lizards, frogs, and birds' eggs. They also eat insects such as bees and young beetles, called grubs. Badgers will also feed on dead animals that they find on the road.

Badger Foods

frog

groundhog

beetle grubs

bee

lizard

chipmunk

ground squirrel

How do you think a badger catches
small animals that live underground?

Digging for Dinner

A badger finds its prey by looking for the entrance to a smaller animal's burrow.

Then the badger starts to dig into the underground home with its long claws.

The ground squirrel or chipmunk inside the burrow may try to dig an escape tunnel.

It's no use, though, because the powerful badger can dig very fast.

The badger quickly finds and catches the smaller animal in its own home!

Sometimes the burrow of a ground squirrel or chipmunk may have two holes. The badger blocks up one hole with soil or rocks so its prey can't escape. Then the badger begins its attack at the other hole.

ground squirrel

Baby Badgers

Adult badgers usually live alone.

In the fall, however, males and females meet up and **mate**.

In spring, a female digs a burrow and makes a soft bed of grass inside.

Here she gives birth to between one and five babies, which are called kits.

At first, the kits' eyes are closed, and they cannot see.

The mother badger feeds the tiny babies milk from her body.

mother badger

three-day-old kit

A newborn badger kit weighs about 3 ounces (85 g). That's the same weight as 15 quarters.

Life in the Burrow

A mother badger spends her days cuddled up with her kits in the burrow.

At night, she leaves the babies safe underground and goes outside to find food.

After about four weeks, the babies' eyes open, and they can see.

When the kits are six weeks old, they leave the burrow for the first time.

They are now big enough to follow their mother when she goes hunting at night.

six-week-old kits

When a female badger has young kits, she uses the same burrow for several weeks. Once the kits start to go outside, the family may move from burrow to burrow.

kits

a mother badger sniffing for food

Growing Up

Baby badgers begin to eat meat when they are about six weeks old.

The mother badger catches small animals and gives them to her babies.

The kits still drink their mother's milk, though, until they are about 12 weeks old.

When they are about five months old, they are ready to leave their mother.

Each young badger goes off on its own to begin its grown-up life.

a young badger digging a burrow

A female badger has her first babies when she is one to two years old. Badgers usually live for five to ten years.

an adult badger peeking out of its burrow in winter

Science Lab

Spot the Badger

Imagine you are a scientist that studies badgers.

Badgers live in the same areas as raccoons, groundhogs, and opossums.

These animals are often a similar shape or color as badgers.

| badger | raccoon | groundhog | opossum |

Scientists must be able to identify an animal—even if they only spot a little of the creature.

Which of these pictures shows a badger? What animal is shown in each of the other pictures?

A   B   C   D

(The answers are on page 24.)

Science Words

burrow (BUR-oh)
a hole or tunnel dug by
an animal for it to live in

mate (MAYT) to come
together in order to have
young

nocturnal
(nok-TUR-nuhl)
active mainly at night

prairies (PRAIR-eez)
large areas of flat land
covered with grass

prey (PRAY) an animal
that is hunted by other
animals for food

23

Index

Read More

Diaz, Katacha. *Badger at Sandy Ridge Road* (*Smithsonian's Backyard*). Norwalk, CT: Palm Kids (2005).

Howard, Fran. *Badgers: Active at Night* (*The Wild World of Animals*). Mankato MN: Capstone (2005).

Sebastian, Emily. *Badgers* (*Animals Underground*). New York: PowerKids Press (2011).

Learn More Online

To learn more about badgers, visit **www.bearportpublishing.com/TheHoleTruth**

Answers

Answers to the activity on page 22

- A is a raccoon
- B is a groundhog
- C is an opossum
- D is a badger

About the Author

Dee Phillips lives near the ocean on the southwest coast of England. She writes nonfiction and fiction books for children. Dee's biggest ambition is to one day walk the entire coast of Britain—it will take about ten months!